HEALTH
and
HYGIENE

Troll Associates

HEALTH
and
HYGIENE

by Rae Bains

Illustrated by Nancy Zink-White

Troll Associates

Library of Congress Cataloging in Publication Data

Bains, Rae.
   Health and hygiene.

   Summary: Explains how proper nutrition, physical
exercise, cleanliness, and rest contribute to building
a healthy body.
     1. Health—Juvenile literature. 2. Hygiene—Juvenile
literature. [1. Health. 2. Hygiene. 3. Nutrition]
I. Zink-White, Nancy, ill. II. Title.
RA777.B33   1984   613   84-2627
ISBN 0-8167-0180-6 (lib. bdg.)
ISBN 0-8167-0181-4 (pbk.)

Copyright © 1985 by Troll Associates, Mahwah, New Jersey
All rights reserved. No part of this book may be used
or reproduced in any manner whatsoever without written
permission from the publisher.
Printed in the United States of America

10 9 8 7 6 5 4 3 2 1

Healthy people enjoy life from the moment they get up in the morning until the moment they fall asleep at night. They have plenty of energy to learn and work and play. They feel good about themselves, and they feel good about everything and everybody around them. So it makes sense for everyone to take care of his or her health.

Good health starts with a well-balanced diet. That's because your body needs the nutrients supplied by many different foods. These nutrients help you to grow, they give you energy, they help your body to resist disease and to repair cells, and they keep you strong. The nutrients you need are proteins, vitamins, minerals, fats, and carbohydrates.

As you grow, your body needs a constant supply of protein. That's because each cell in your body is made up largely of proteins. And since each cell lives only a short while, your body must continue to build new cells all the time to replace the ones that are dying.

There is a great deal of protein in meat, fish, poultry, eggs, cheese, milk, peanut butter, beans, and many kinds of grains. So when you eat these foods, you are giving your body an important kind of nutrient.

Your body also needs a constant supply of vitamins. There are many different kinds of vitamins, and some of them have strange names, like riboflavin, pyridoxine, and ascorbic acid. But they also have shorter names, like vitamin B_2, vitamin B_6, and vitamin C.

Different vitamins are found in different kinds of foods. Vitamin A is found in fish-liver oils, in yellow fruits, and in dark green vegetables. It helps build strong bones and healthy skin. It also helps promote the healing of cuts and scrapes and helps maintain good eyesight.

The eight B vitamins help to keep the eyes, skin, and mouth healthy, as well as the brain and nervous system. They also aid in digestion. The B vitamins are found in beans and in whole grains, as well as in vitamin-enriched grains.

Vitamin C, which is found in citrus fruits and some vegetables, helps the body to heal wounds and to build healthy blood vessels, bones, and teeth. Since extra vitamin C cannot be stored in the body, foods containing vitamin C should be eaten every day.

Eggs, butter, liver, and milk provide us with vitamin D. This important vitamin helps build strong bones and teeth.

There are two other important vitamins —E and K. Vitamin E helps keep cell tissue strong, and Vitamin K helps your blood to clot. Vitamins E and K are found in many kinds of food; so any well-balanced diet will provide them in sufficient amounts.

In addition to proteins and vitamins, a well-balanced diet will also provide all the minerals your body needs. Minerals, such as calcium, phosphorous, and potassium, help your body to build muscles, bones, and tissues.

You also need fats and carbohydrates, or starches, in your diet to give you energy. Carbohydrates and fats are your body's fuel supply. They give you the energy to run and jump and learn, just as gasoline provides the energy to run a car's engine.

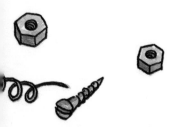

The energy in the food you eat is measured in units called calories. Different foods contain different amounts of calories. You must take in enough calories every day, in the food you eat, to satisfy your body's needs. If you take in more calories than your body can burn up, the extra calories are stored as body fat, and you will gain weight. If you do not take in as many calories as your body needs, the stored fat is used as fuel, and you will lose weight.

And if you take in the same number of calories as your body burns up, your weight should remain the same. Of course, the number of calories your body burns up depends on many factors, including your age, sex, and how active you happen to be.

Besides eating the right amounts of the right kinds of food, you should also drink plenty of water. Water is not a nutrient, but it carries nutrients to all of the body's cells. It also helps the body get rid of waste matter. So water is a very important part of anyone's diet.

A balanced diet should include every kind of nutrient. To simplify planning a balanced diet, nutritionists divide foods into different groups. One system divides foods into four basic groups. They are the milk group, the meat group, the bread and cereals group, and the fruits and vegetables group.

Another system divides foods into seven groups. Group 1 includes meat, poultry, fish, eggs, dried beans, peas, and nuts. Group 2 includes leafy, green, and yellow vegetables. Group 3 includes citrus fruits, tomatoes, lettuce, and raw cabbage. Group 4 includes potatoes and noncitrus fruits. Group 5 is made up of bread, cereals, and flour. Group 6 consists of butter and margarine to which vitamin A has been added. And Group 7 includes milk and other milk products.

19

Of course, proper diet isn't the only key to good health. You also need exercise. Physical activity helps to burn up the calories you take in. If you sit around doing nothing, your body uses less than one hundred calories in an hour. If you run or swim, you use more than three times as many calories!

Physical activity helps your body in other ways, too. It keeps your muscles healthy and strong. That gives you good posture, which, in turn, makes you look good. Physical activity also helps your coordination. When you have good coordination, it means your muscles work together smoothly. You need good coordination to hit a ball, dance, roller skate—or even to write a letter.

Exercise also helps the inside of your body. It does this by keeping the blood vessels open, so your blood can flow easily to every part of your body. Healthy blood vessels become even more important as you grow older. But don't wait until you are grown up to form good exercise habits. Running, swimming, cycling, skating, and playing tennis are some of the sports that can last a lifetime and which you can start doing right now.

After a day filled with nutritious food and plenty of activity, you should be ready for some sleep. That's good, because getting enough sleep is an important part of health and hygiene. Different people need different amounts of sleep. Some people may feel rested after six hours of sleep; others may need twelve hours. Most school-age youngsters need eight to ten hours of sleep a night.

While you sleep, your body builds up energy for the next day. Your muscles relax, your breathing slows, your cells repair themselves, and your blood carries away body wastes.

But even while you sleep, your brain is busy. It is busy dreaming. Scientists have found that people become cranky, nervous, and unable to work well if they don't have enough dream-time. And since you cannot dream unless you are asleep, you need enough sleep to be relaxed, happy, and healthy.

Keeping healthy also means keeping clean. Keeping clean helps remove germs that can cause disease. When you brush your teeth after every meal, you remove food particles on which bacteria feed. These bacteria cause tooth decay and gum disease. Brushing is just part of a good dental-hygiene program. You should also visit a dentist two or three times a year for a checkup, for a tooth-cleaning, and to have necessary dental work done.

Everyone should also keep his or her skin clean to prevent disease and infection caused by harmful bacteria. Bacteria are always present on the skin, but washing with soap and water keeps the bacteria out of cuts and scrapes. A shower at least once a day washes away dirt, perspiration, and oils that can clog the tiny skin openings called pores.

Keeping your hair and nails clean serves two purposes. It keeps the scalp and fingers from becoming infected, and it keeps them looking neat and clean.

Healthy eyes and ears enable you to see and hear what's going on all around. How can you keep them healthy?

Let's start with your eyes. You can protect them from injury by never looking directly at the sun. The sun is so bright that its rays could cause permanent damage. And be sure there's enough light when you are reading or watching television. Of course, regular checkups by an eye doctor can help locate any problems, so they can be corrected quickly.

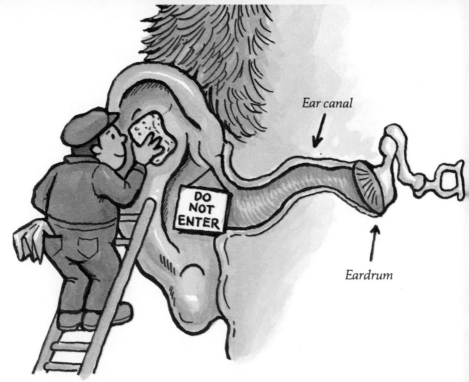

Ear canal

Eardrum

DO NOT ENTER

What about your ears? Keep them clean, of course, by washing them, but never put anything into your ear canal. At the end of the ear canal is a sensitive tissue called the eardrum. To avoid damaging it, wash only the outside part of the ear—the visible part. If you have a problem with your ears, such as an earache, the build-up of ear wax, or difficulty in hearing, you should see a doctor.

Healthy people who take good care of themselves don't need much medical attention. But even the healthiest person should have regular medical checkups and should have all of the recommended inoculations.

These help to build up a resistance to such diseases as measles, polio, smallpox, diphtheria, and tetanus. It is much wiser— and easier—to prevent an illness than to have to be cured of it!

Of course, everyone should avoid tobacco, alcohol, and drugs. The only time anyone should take medicine of any kind is when it has been prescribed by a doctor.

Remember—you have only one body, and it has to last you a lifetime. So it makes good sense to take the best care of it you can!